Perspectives on
Shared Reading

Perspectives on Shared Reading

PLANNING AND PRACTICE

Bobbi Fisher

and

Emily Fisher Medvic

Heinemann

Portsmouth, NH

Heinemann
A division of Reed Elsevier Inc.
361 Hanover Street
Portsmouth, NH 03801–3912
www.heinemann.com

Offices and agents throughout the world

Library of Congress Cataloging-in-Publication Data
CIP data is on file with the Library of Congress.
ISBN 0-325-00215-0

Editor: Leigh Peake
Production: Abigail M. Heim
Cover design: Jenny Jensen Greenleaf
Cover illustration: Lynn Jeffery
Manufacturing: Louise Richardson

Printed in the United States of America on acid-free paper
03   02   01   00   DA   3   4   5

for Jim: BF

for Dad: EFM

Contents

Introduction

Bobbi and Emily

As mother and daughter we have spent almost thirty years talking about books together. It is from our love of teaching and learning through literature that we have written this book for both new and experienced teachers. Although its primary audience is pre-K through grade-two teachers, we believe that teachers of grades three through six will find many useful strategies that they can adapt to their classrooms. This book describes our thinking about and planning for shared reading, and our classroom experiences practicing it.

Bobbi

The first time I saw a big book used with children was at a kindergarten conference in Boston in the fall of 1984. I had heard that an interesting man from New Zealand by the name of Don Holdaway was going to demonstrate the use of big books with a group of second graders who had come to the conference with their teacher. My attendance at that session changed my teaching career forever.

The following spring I took a course from Don on emergent and beginning reading. He lent me *Hairy Bear* (Cowley), and I began to start every day in my kindergarten with shared reading. When I moved to teach first grade, shared reading continued as the foundation of my teaching and the children's learning.

As I began to understand the importance for learning literacy of the bedtime story at home, and its correlation to shared reading in school, I realized the pursuit of learning that occurred when I read bedtime stories to my own two children, Tim and Emily (who are now doing the same every night with their own children).

As a little girl Emily spent hours playing school and reading to her stuffed animals at home. In my classroom she helped sort books, blocks, and crayons and tidy up after school, and then when she was in high school she wrote charts, made games, and created name tags and bulletin boards for my kindergarteners. Thus, it is not surprising that she now has an elementary classroom of her own, putting into practice in her individual way many of the ideas that she had helped me develop, and adapting them to the current educational climate.

The idea of writing this book came to me as I talked with Emily about her master's thesis on shared reading and her experience as a beginning teacher. It occurred to me that a small, accessible book on the subject would be helpful to teachers wanting to practice shared reading in their classrooms and to find ways to integrate it into their existing curriculum. I also realized that Emily has something to offer that a seasoned teacher like myself can't provide. She knows what would be helpful to teachers, new and experienced, who are learning about shared reading for the first time.

She also knows how the current atmosphere surrounding standards and testing directly affect the teaching and learning in classrooms, and she has figured out ways to include shared reading in the standards/testing climate. This was something I never had to address, for when I retired from classroom teaching in 1994, standards and testing were just beginning to be discussed, and they didn't influence my teaching or classroom community.

I was also observing that shared reading, an essential foundation of literacy in primary classrooms, was being neglected. When I spoke with teachers at conferences about this, they told me that due to curriculum demands, which focused on isolated skills and pervasive pressures to teach to state standards and testing, they weren't certain they should devote the necessary thirty to forty-five minutes a day to shared reading. This concerned me, since I feel that shared reading is one of the most efficient and successful ways to engage children in rigorous learning and to teach skills in the context of meaningful literature. I shared my concerns with Emily and we agreed to write this book.

Emily

One of my favorite activities as a child was to take the big bag of books that my mother and I had selected from the library, line up all of my stuffed animals, and read out loud to them. I remember reading, showing the pictures, talking about the stories, rereading, asking questions, and then writing my own stories. However, I mostly remember loving books.

My memory of children's books and the love of reading eventually led me to a career my mother had so obviously enjoyed. I had spent many hours in her classroom and at home helping her get things ready for school. I remember when she began to accumulate "big books" she experienced a renewed passion in her teaching.

When I began studying for my master's degree, I had an idea of what I wanted to do in my classroom. First on my list was shared reading. I was not aware of the adapting and adjusting I would have to do to accommodate standardized testing, but I knew the importance of the model, and I believed in it. I developed a proposal for my thesis and set off to analyze my teaching through shared reading. With shared reading, the children were interested and learning the skills and strategies for reading and writing, as well as the content areas of social studies and science. At the same time, I was becoming more confident—a better, more effective, and happier teacher.

I am one of the most fortunate beginning teachers. I can always call my mother to tell her about what has gone well, talk out difficulties, ask questions, or simply be reassured. She has guided me while insisting that I follow my own beliefs and instincts. Anyone who has heard her speak knows that she truly values what teachers know and do. When I told her about the pressures of standards and testing, she listened to my ideas and gave feedback and suggestions. I am convinced that I can teach the standards with shared reading—not only effectively, but also meaningfully and with joy.

Bobbi and Emily

This book is composed of two sections. Bobbi wrote Section One from her teaching perspective of twenty-five years. Chapter One addresses the theories underlying shared reading. It discusses the similarities as well as the differences between the conditions of the bedtime story and Holdaway's Natural Learning Classroom Model, of which shared reading is a major part. Chapters Two and Three, also written by Bobbi, draw upon her years of experience as a classroom teacher, and her current experiences planning and practicing shared reading with teachers and students in classrooms throughout the country.

In Section Two, Emily writes from her perspective of a beginning teacher. In Chapter Four she details how she plans for shared reading and describes some of the materials and their uses that she has found helpful. In Chapter Five she describes in more detail how she puts her planning into practice.

Part One

Perspectives of an Experienced Teacher

1

Shared Reading and the Bedtime Story

Shared reading is a time when the entire class gathers together to share a variety of literacy experiences by reading and discussing a variety of texts. Many of the texts are enlarged so that all the children can see the print and pictures and thus talk more easily about them. Shared reading is a noncompetitive time when children of different abilities and experiences learn from and with each other.

A daily shared reading time in primary classrooms supports the foundations of literacy teaching and learning for all children. It continues and builds on the literacy started at home with the bedtime story, and it helps children develop a love of learning as they learn about literacy and learn to read. It involves rigorous teaching and learning, and provides models for extending these literacy experiences to practice and sharing times throughout the day. It also promotes community and builds self-esteem (see Figure 1–1).

The Natural Learning Classroom Model

The model of shared reading comes from Don Holdaway's (1979) work with primary children in the Auckland, New Zealand, public schools in the 1970s. As he observed children who came to school already reading or who were close to reading independently, he asked, "What are the conditions that enable these children to read, and how can teachers apply these conditions to the classroom setting?" Holdaway observed that these early readers had consistently been read to at home by a caring adult, usually a parent (a bonded adult); they had spent time by themselves practicing reading; and

Shared reading:

- Supports the foundations of literacy learning
- Builds on literacy started at home
- Develops a love of learning
- Helps children learn to read
- Involves rigorous teaching and learning
- Provides literacy models for children to practice
- Builds community
- Builds self-esteem

Figure 1–1   Shared Reading

they had opportunities to perform as readers to those important adults in their lives.

Holdaway applied these optimal home conditions to the classroom setting and developed a Natural Learning Classroom Model (see Figure 1–2), which includes *demonstration, participation, practice/role-play,* and *performance.* Shared reading, when the teacher *demonstrates* and the children *participate* in literacy experiences, corresponds to the bedtime story, when the parent reads and the child joins in by commenting, questioning, and reading along. *Practice/role-play* corresponds to the times in the home when the child is playing by himself or herself or with siblings or friends without the attention of an adult. The child takes the role of different people and characters he or she has observed or read about. Playing house and playing school are examples of this time. In school, *practice/role-play* includes the various times in the day when children are working independently and practicing the literacy skills and strategies they experienced during shared reading. Names for these times include *choice time, dramatic play, work time, reading workshop, writing workshop,* and *inquiry time.*

Finally, children receive opportunities to *perform* or share their newly discovered competencies with others. At home children ask to read to their parents and show parents their writing and drawings. In school children read to the class or to their friends, share their writing by sitting in the author's chair, dramatize a story, post

	School	Home
Demonstration	Shared reading	Bedtime story
Participation	Shared reading	Bedtime story
Practice/role-play	Choice time	Play time
	Dramatic play	Playing alone
	Work time	Playing with a friend
	Reading workshop	Playing house
	Writing workshop	Playing school
	Workshop time	
	Inquiry time	
Performance	Sharing time	Many different times
	Reading to others	Bedtime story
	Author's chair	Showing what they can do
	Posting work	
	Publishing	Reading to others throughout the day
	Dramatizing a story	Play time
		Writing lists, thank-you notes, stories

Figure 1–2 Natural Learning Classroom Model

their work on the bulletin board, or publish for a wider audience (see Figure 1–2).

Applying the Conditions of the Bedtime Story to Shared Reading

As we refine our classroom teaching, it is useful to reexamine the conditions of the bedtime story and analyze how we can apply them to shared reading, taking into account the different dynamics involved in reading to one child at home versus twenty to thirty children in a group setting at school (see Figure 1–3).

- Cozy, positive experience
- Child sees and touches the text
- Child participates in the reading
- Approximations are valued
- Child chooses what to read
- Reading a variety of texts
- Reading the same text over and over again
- Texts have deep meaning
- Texts have memorable language

Figure 1–3 Conditions of the Bedtime Story and Shared Reading

Cozy, Positive Experience

The *bedtime story* experience is always positive, as parent and child enjoy themselves together. Adjectives describing this time include *humorous, playful, relaxed, respectful,* and *cozy.* Usually the two sit close together. If they are reading on a couch, the parent might have one arm around the child, or the child might be sitting on the parent's lap. If the child is in bed, the parent might be sitting or lying on the bed, or sitting in a chair close by.

Although parents introduce the idea of the bedtime story and take an active part in reading to the child, they do not control everything that goes on. They offer their reading, interests, and time and follow the child's lead. Parent and child interact, but the child's interests, pacing, and attention to detail dominate. There is no need for discipline or punishment. If the child becomes restless with a story, parents pick a new one. If the child gets too active, parents terminate the session and get some physical exercise.

In our classroom, *shared reading* is also a positive experience, with the teacher and children enjoying the time together. Like the parent at home, the teacher becomes the bonded adult in school. She sits on a chair next to her teaching easel, which displays charts and big books, and the children sit on the floor close to her. The teacher selects some of the texts and keeps in mind certain skills and strategies to teach, but as they read, she also follows the children's leads. She accepts the comments and approximations of all the children and is skilled in positive teaching. If the group gets restless, she might include a text that allows for dramatization, such as *The Gingerbread Man* (Parkes and Smith), or movement, such as "Lou, Lou, Skip to My Lou."

There are some important differences, however, between the bedtime story and shared reading. At home, the story is usually between one child and one adult, allowing the child full participation and individual attention. In school, the children are learning in a community. The teacher strives to involve them all and meet their individual needs, but she knows that she cannot always accomplish this. Her challenge is to keep the experience positive and engaging when several children want different stories, when one child wants to talk all the time, or when another child is having difficulty being part of the group.

It should be noted that when more than one child is involved in the bedtime story, the situation more closely resembles a shared reading setting in which children with different abilities and interests are learning together. One of the benefits of shared reading is that as the children learn about literacy, they learn to work together as a group of caring, respectful human beings.

Child Sees and Touches the Text

When parent and child sit close together during the *bedtime story*, both can see and touch the text. The child learns how to hold and manipulate a book and initiates and reinforces learning by touching and pointing to the print and pictures. The parent comments as he points, "Look, Samantha, there's a word that begins with an S, the same letter that your name begins with." Samantha also points, and the next day she initiates the game by pointing to an S in another book. She continues to take control by turning the pages and pointing to other print conventions. Then one day she puts the book on her lap and announces, "Now, I'm going to read to you."

During *shared reading* it is essential that all the children see the text. The letters must be clearly written and large enough for everyone to see, and there must be a clear line of vision, especially for those sitting toward the back or at the side of the group. The children should have many opportunities to observe the teacher demonstrate conventions of print through various pointing and masking techniques, and be given opportunities to come up and touch the text and pictures themselves.

The opportunities to touch the text during the bedtime story and shared reading vary in immediacy and amount. In the bedtime story, the child immediately can touch the detail in question and no permission is needed. The touch can start as a motor activity, not solely as a verbal response. There is no delay between the desire to respond and the response itself. In shared reading, the children usually must wait to be called on to come up to the text. Sometimes by the time they get there they have forgotten their response or have lost their place. Since children have infrequent chances individually to touch the text, it is especially important that they have daily opportunities to read the big books and charts on their own during practice time.

Child Participates in the Reading

During the *bedtime story*, the child continually participates in the reading in a variety of ways, such as talking about the pictures, commenting on the story, repeating memorable words and phrases, reading along, and turning the pages. There is a playfulness about it all, with the parent and child enjoying the dialogue. It is conversational in tone and substance.

The teacher tries to replicate this aspect during *shared reading*. As she reads, the children participate. She encourages them to read along, invites them to complete a sentence by letting her voice drop at the end of a line, asks open-ended questions, and encourages the children to comment and respond in the group.

Approximations Are Valued

The parent is aware that the child's reading-like behavior, with its many approximations, parallels the way that he learned to talk. The child tried out language to get his needs met, and over time his talk increasingly resembled conventional speech. Instead of correcting the child, the parent responded with natural conversation, extending and elaborating the language and accepting with assurance the child's developing language. Thus the child's confidence and self-esteem remained strong. As the child participates during the bedtime story, the parent responds positively to his reading approximations. The parent doesn't correct the child but notices that over time the child self-corrects when something doesn't make sense.

Teachers understand the parallels between learning to talk and learning to read. Many are familiar with Cambourne's (1988) conditions of learning to talk (immersion, demonstration, engagement, expectation, responsibility, approximations, practice, and feedback) and apply them to the classroom setting, particularly during shared reading and when they work with individual readers. Teachers create an environment in which children feel free to take risks and approximate as they work toward accuracy. Teachers also see the value of these approximations and accompanying self-corrections as essential strategies of the reading process. They notice that approximations vary with each reader and that the shared reading setting provides many opportunities for each child to approximate and self-correct during group reading.

Child Chooses What to Read

Although both the parent and child choose reading materials for the *bedtime story*, the child ultimately agrees to what they will read. In collaboration, they might buy books together, make selections at the library, or pick books from the child's bookshelf. Once the story time begins, the child chooses which books to read, which ones to read again and again, and when not to finish a story, and the parent complies.

In *shared reading*, the teacher takes more direct control than the parent over what is being read. He has to balance the interests and reading needs of all the children, and meet a wide variety of curriculum requirements. He gives the children as much text choice as possible and listens carefully to their interests.

Reading a Variety of Texts

During the *bedtime story* the parent and child read a variety of texts. Although storybooks are the most popular genre, the parent also introduces information books, poetry, magazines, encyclopedias, and newspapers. Parents also make available different books that reflect the interests of the child. If they are going to take a family trip in the car to visit relatives, they might read books about car travel and visiting. If the child has been intrigued with the giraffes at the zoo, they might read stories about giraffes as well as information books about them.

At *shared reading* time, the teacher introduces different texts: storybooks, information books, informational storybooks, poetry, and biographies in a variety of genres. She knows stories that are popular with the age group she is teaching; she includes books that are part of the school-wide curriculum; she finds texts that respond to the interests of individual children; and she includes subjects that are interesting to her.

Reading the Same Text Over and Over Again

During the *bedtime story*, children ask to hear their favorite stories over and over again and the parent complies. These stories address the important themes in children's lives and resonate with memorable language. With each reading the child delves more deeply into the meaning of the story, as well as assimilates the visual and auditory language of the text. The same thing happens during *shared reading* when the children and teacher read favorite books over and over again.

Texts Have Deep Meaning

A story becomes a favorite because its meaning has value to the child. On the surface level, children relate to the story because they identify strongly with the characters, setting, or subject and/or because they want to learn more about them. On a deeper level, favorite bedtime stories speak to the developmental issues of the reader; each time children hear the same story, they gain new meaning and insights about their life. For example, issues concerning parental love are addressed in *Are You My Mother?* (Eastman); reality and fantasy in *No More Jumping on the Bed* (Arnold); power and control in *Mortimer* (Munsch); and security and fear in *Goodnight Moon* (Brown). *Where The Wild Things Are* (Sendak) addresses all of these developmental issues.

Texts Have Memorable Language

Favorite stories have memorable language that children love to hear again and again. Initially the children are attracted to the rhythm and rhyme in a text, and with repeated oral exposure they begin to memorize these patterns of written language and repeat them while reading along. They follow the text visually as the parent or teacher points word for word, and over time they begin to match the words on the page with what they have remembered. This memory supports them in this stage of word matching so they can concentrate on the graphophonics. Children become more accurate and more fluent with each reading.

The bedtime story propels children into literacy. Children who have been read to at home come to school with a developing understanding of literacy and a love of reading, and shared reading simulates and enhances this important experience. Holdaway discovered that daily shared reading was an optimal way to build everyone's storehouse of familiar stories, and that during this group learning time all the children were participating at their developmental level.

> *The major purpose from the parent's point of view is to give pleasure. . . . From the child's point of view the situation is among the happiest and most secure in his experience. The stories themselves are enriching and deeply satisfying. . . . Thus the child develops strongly positive associations with the flow of story language and with the physical characteristics of the books.*
> *(Holdaway 1979, 39, 40)*

2

Building Community

Shared reading builds self-esteem and a sense of community as it leads children into literacy. When children feel good about themselves and recognize that they are valued members of the classroom, it is easier for them to learn to read and write, *and* they develop a love of learning, as well. Literacy learning, self-confidence, caring for each other, and the love of learning go hand in hand.

When I am in a classroom, I believe it is my responsibility to set a positive atmosphere for learning, and that my students gain confidence in their ability as learners when there is an absence of academic competition. Applying Holdaway's Natural Learning Classroom Model to kindergarten and first-grade classrooms, I try to establish a noncompetitive community of learners during shared reading by treating each child as a unique learner and valued human being. Together the children participate in the community as they learn to read. This collaborative, trusting atmosphere continues during practice time as they confidently explore new literacy learning through reading, writing, dramatic play, art projects, and constructing with blocks, either alone or with friends. This model invites them to learn from each other as well as from me.

Creating Community Through Song

Teachers across the country encourage singing as a way to build community in their classrooms. Many believe that group singing is one of the most unifying classroom activities because it entices and enables children of all backgrounds, cultures, first-language abilities, and interests to participate together. Singing draws *everyone* in.

Strategies for Including Everyone

Song, as a signal to begin group time, ensures that we start each day as a community of learners. As we finish settling in for the day, I begin to sing, a signal to the class that we are ready to start group time and that everyone should come to the rug area. There is a joyful ease as throughout the room children unite in song as they finish what they are doing and join the group to begin our formal learning time. Children arrive at the group singing together rather than talking privately, and they focus on a shared text of the song rather than on individual interests. We aren't waiting for the children who are late coming to the group. We begin with the learning, and the latecomers join when they are ready. Although it is important that all the children are present to hear the beginning, middle, and end of any story that we read and discuss, they can still benefit from the singing even if they miss part of a song.

This easing in is very respectful of children. Those who are ready should not have to sit and wait; their time shouldn't be wasted; they should be learning. The latecomers may have good reasons why they can't get there right away, and they also should be respected. Their bus may have been late, they may have had trouble unzipping their jackets, or they may move at a slower pace than others. Knowing that the entire group isn't waiting for them reduces unnecessary anxiety.

Beginning group time with singing also breaks the pattern of waiting for that one child who is always the last to join the group each day. Otherwise, the rest of the class may sense your impatience and join in your annoyance. The late child then becomes an outsider, and being "on time" becomes the criteria for membership in the shared reading community, instead of being a participant in a harmonized joy of literacy learning. This fractured community can continue throughout the rest of the day and build throughout the years both for the ostracized child and the rest of the class.

The breakdown of community is particularly poignant for children who have difficulty being members of a group or who (consciously or unconsciously) continuously disrupt it. Children who previously have received negative attention while the class waited find that we are going on with joyful learning without them, but that we are ready to include them when they are ready to join us. My focus is on learning, not behavior, and they have the choice to join or remain outside the group. Singing is compelling and almost always draws them in. Most children would rather sing and be part of the community than isolate themselves in another part of the room.

Selecting Songs

Various criteria go into selecting songs for shared reading. Originally, I started by picking songs with tunes that I knew and liked and wrote the words on charts. This way I could use the song before I knew the words by heart. I also went to the local library. Looking through songbooks, I was surprised at the number of songs I knew. I also borrowed song tapes from the library or from friends, and on my way to school listened for ones I liked and/or knew. I collected songs with themes of friendship, respect, and self-esteem, as well as songs that celebrate diverse cultures. I tried to note songs that related to our social studies and science curriculum, and kept in mind the interests and cultural backgrounds of individual children in my class. I included funny and serious, lively and slow, and sad and happy songs. (See Figure 2–1.)

Our students are also an excellent resource for songs and can contribute raps, ethnic music, and songs written in their first language. I encourage my students to bring tapes from home. I find out what kinds of music they like and incorporate their songs into our classroom repertoire. Teachers can write the words on a chart and ask the students who bring the songs to decorate it with pictures and highlight special words they want to share.

Children enjoy being asked to be the teacher and to teach one of their favorite songs to the class. Students who are reluctant to join the group or who ask for extra attention during group time might benefit from leading the class in song. When students become teachers, the Natural Learning Classroom Model is complete. Children become the demonstrators as they perform what they have learned.

Do I have songs . . .

- I like?
- from anthologies?
- from trade books?
- from big books?
- with tapes?
- with themes of friendship, respect, and self-esteem?
- that celebrate diverse cultures?
- that reflect the cultures and first languages of my students?
- that relate to our social studies and science curriculum?
- that are funny and serious, lively and slow, and sad and happy?
- that my students bring from home?
- to dance and move to?

Figure 2–1   Things to Keep in Mind When Selecting Songs . . .

Creating Community Through Discussion

As a literacy teacher, one of my goals is to help students become critical readers and writers for a variety of meaningful purposes. Discussions of texts are at the heart of shared reading, and in order for all students to participate, they must feel safe to take risks and say what they are really thinking, not what they know is a safe response. This includes trying out ideas that they are forming, ideas that they are not certain of, ideas that are not typical within the classroom, and ideas that challenge the status quo.

Strategies for Including Everyone

Creating an atmosphere in which all the children feel safe to speak lays the foundation for meaningful discussion. One good strategy is to receive comments by acknowledging that you heard them without giving any value judgment or specific comment. For example, in introducing the humorous book *The Scrubbing Machine* (Cowley), I asked a group of children what they thought a scrubbing machine might do. I received each remark by nodding my head; then I moved on to the next child. At first only a few children were willing to contribute, but as they observed that all ideas were accepted equally, more were willing to take a risk and share their predictions. The children were learning that I was interested in their ideas, not in a right answer, and that we weren't playing the game "Guess what's in the teacher's head?"

Sometimes, however, I want to build upon a child's comment. I continue to hear what everyone has to say, and then I return to discuss a particular point. Other times I ask a child to elaborate and then turn the discussion over to the group. I don't respond with, "Aren't you clever to have come up with such a creative thought," or "My, you are smart." Such comments destroy the learning community by encouraging arrogance in the "smart" child, separating the "creative" child from the rest of the group, and diminishing the confidence of the child who doesn't come up with creative ideas that the teacher seems to like.

Focusing on the ideas, not on the personality of a child, unleashes the creative thinking of all the children and encourages the group to generate and develop new understandings. It allows for many people to think and discuss together to create ideas. The children create a learning community when they share ideas and think together.

Critical Literacy

The ways that teachers initiate and sustain class discussions shape the character of our classroom community. If we want a learning atmosphere in which students explore ideas, form concepts, discuss variant points of view, experience empathy, and critique their environment and the world in which they live, we must open up discussion and become co-learners.

Therefore, I often initiate conversations with my own wondering statements. For example, when I introduced *The Scrubbing Machine* I asked, "I wonder what a scrubbing machine could do? I wonder what will happen with the scrubbing machine to make this an interesting story? I wonder where Joy Cowley got the idea for this story? I wonder how the story might be different if a man were running the machine instead of Mrs. Wishy-Washy?" I also asked factual questions, not to test the children but to set the context for critical discussions. Their responses to such questions as "What is a scrubbing machine? What do vacuum cleaners pick up?" fostered further dialogue and critique.

Together, the children and I became critical meaning makers as these conversations continued and developed into significant and honest discussions. We learned new information; we increased our information base; we shared ideas; we listened and debated; we changed our minds; we held to our opinions; and we came to consensus. Through meaningful discussions, we built a classroom community in which we pursued rigorous learning, increased our information base, learned new skills and strategies, valued diverse ideas, and respected others. (See Figure 2–2.)

Creating Community and Learning to Read

When I work with students in early childhood classrooms, one of my jobs is to help them become independent readers and writers. Children develop this autonomy during the early years of schooling, and acquiring skills and strategies is part of the process. Although we can outline a general learning progression, children develop literacy in their own unique ways, and teachers must offer opportunities for them to gain this independence. Shared reading

---

Elements of literacy discussions:

- Engaging in significant and honest dialogue
- Sharing ideas
- Listening and debating
- Changing our minds
- Holding to our opinions
- Coming to consensus
- Valuing diverse ideas
- Respecting others
- Experiencing empathy
- Critiquing the world in which we live

Figure 2–2 Literacy Discussions

(accompanied by independent practice and one-on-one focused teaching) provides this experience because it demonstrates a wide variety of skills and strategies that children can select, try out, accept, reject, self-correct, and confirm. It also allows students time to experiment with these skills and strategies at their own pace.

Developing Skills and Strategies in Context

Shared reading helps the children acquire the skills and strategies they need to understand a text and become independent, confident readers. I teach skills (isolated units of knowledge) and strategies (patterns of learning) in context so students can easily transfer them to use in their own independent reading. For example, when children reread *The Scrubbing Machine* independently after shared reading, they might approach the word *machine* by saying the sound /m/ and looking at the picture to help them figure out the word. They would be applying the skill of the letter-sound correspondence strategically in a meaningful way. Their understanding of the word *machine* and their knowledge and application of the /m/ would encourage them to keep reading with comprehension.

Shared reading provides emergent and beginning readers with repeated and varied opportunities to observe, discuss, and practice the conventions of print and learn how print works, as detailed in Figure 2–3.

When we read strategically, we integrate the language cueing systems: pragmatic or personal schema, semantic, syntactic, and graphophonemic (see Figure 2–4). My goal during shared reading is to help children read along with ease and understanding. I might ask, "What do you know about the subject of this book?" (pragmatic); "Does this make sense?" (semantic); "Does it sound right?" (syntactic); and "What word is this?" (graphophonemic). I demonstrate different reading strategies, such as rereading, slowing down and pointing, and looking at the pictures.

Understanding and applying the graphophonemic cueing system is an essential component of the reading process and one that develops during these early years of schooling. In school, most children acquire these necessary skills and strategies for successful reading and writing through demonstrations and participation with print during shared reading, and through daily practice during writing time.

Book knowledge

- Front of the book
- Back of the book
- Reading the left-hand page before the right-hand page
- Holding a book and turning the pages
- Distinction between pictures and print
- Title
- Author

Directionality

- Where to start reading on the page
- Reading left to right
- Return sweep
- Page sequence

Visual conventions

- Difference between a letter, word, and sentence
- Spaces between words
- Punctuation (period, question mark, exclamation mark, comma, quotation marks)
- Letter recognition (upper- and lowercase)

Auditory conventions

- Sound-symbol relationship
- Hearing use of punctuation
- One-to-one correspondence
- Intonation (use of punctuation, emphasis on certain words, for example)

Figure 2–3   Conventions of Print

From *Joyful Learning in Kindergarten, Revised Edition* by Bobbi Fisher
Adapted from Marie Clay (1993)

1. *Personal Schema.* Our discussion starts with what the children know, focusing on the experiences and knowledge they bring to the text.
   - What do you know about the topic?
   - Tell about any related experiences you have had.

2. *Semantic Cueing System.* Our focus turns to the meaning of the text we are reading.
   - What do you think the story is about?
   - What do you think will happen next?
   - What do the pictures tell us?
   - Retell the story.
   - What would make sense?
   - Talk about the characters.
   - Talk about the story structure.
   - Compare similarities and differences with other books.
   - What other words could the author have used that would make sense?
   - Finish this line with a word or phrase that would make sense in the poem or story (auditory cloze).

3. *Syntactic Cueing System.* Our focus is on the language, the grammar of the text.
   - Does it sound right?
   - What other words could the author use that would sound right?
   - Finish this line with a word or phrase that would fit the sound of the language of the poem or story (auditory cloze).

Figure 2–4 Language Cueing System
(continues on p. 22)

---

4. *Grapho-phonic Cueing System.* The grapho (letters) and phonic (sounds) are a tool to predict and confirm a word in the text.

- Use the first letter to predict what the word might be.
- Use the first letter(s), last letter, length of word, configuration of word to confirm what the word is.
- Guess what the last word or words in this line could be (auditory cloze).
- Listen to the first sound of this word and predict what it could be (auditory cloze).
- Look at the first letter or letters of this word and predict what it could be (visual cloze).

Figure 2–4 Continued

Children in kindergarten and first grade are familiar with many of the words they hear in a story and are ready to recognize them in print form. According to Moustafa (1997), research shows that although it is difficult for children to analyze spoken words into phonemes (the smallest units of sound in spoken words), children can analyze words into onsets (beginning consonants) and rimes (vowel and consonants) that follow. They do this naturally, without being specifically taught, through oral language. As they learn to read they use this knowledge "to make analogies between familiar and unfamiliar print words to figure out how to say unfamiliar print words" (46). Thus, during shared reading students need many opportunities to listen and play with language.

Strategies for Including Everyone

Some children come to our classrooms as independent readers, able to read texts that they have never heard before. Some have developed what Don Holdaway (1979) calls a Literacy Set and are ready to take off. Others are just beginning to make sense of how print works. We also have students who have not heard many stories or had much experience with books before coming to school. Regardless, it is essential that we create a classroom community in which all the children feel confident to pursue their own way of learning.

Competition among children learning to read breaks down this community, and teachers must do all they can to eliminate it in their classrooms. For example, during shared reading, I don't put children on the spot and signal them out to give a correct answer. Open-ended questions allow all the students to participate at their developmental level as members of the learning community. I try to preface questions with an invitation to the group, rather than a demand to an individual. "Who would like to . . . ?" gives the student the responsibility to choose and take a risk. When we ask, "Who would like to tell us something you notice?" everyone can participate. There is no wrong answer. We get more specific but still leave space for student choice when we ask, "Who would like to find a letter in their name?" or ". . . a three-letter word?" Even when we request a specific answer, such as, "Who would like to show us the word *tree*?" we ask for volunteers.

Much of my teaching during shared reading does not come from my questioning, but from our reading and singing together. Although they are responding in unison, the children are each working at their individual developmental levels (Fisher 1998). Independent readers watch how a word is spelled, while children at the level of naming letters might be observing a letter they have just learned. At the same time, everyone is committing the text to deep memory, gaining fluency, constructing meaning, and learning what they need to know about how print and texts work.

> *We find that corporate experiences of culturally significant language have always been powerful modes of learning. . . . If we are to avail ourselves of such vital learning energy, the most important insight we must carry over into the school from these models is that cultural learnings are non-competitive. . . . If we can achieve this corporate spirit, there is no reason why a large class cannot learn together. (Holdaway 1979, 64)*

3

Planning and Practice

Planning

Time in the Day

Shared reading is a time when I demonstrate reading and writing skills and strategies using meaningful, interesting books as the children participate in these literacy experiences. It gives them the foundation for practice times throughout the day when they engage in silent reading, paired reading, guided reading, literature circles, response journals, book sharing, one-on-one reading with the teacher, and writing workshop (see Figure 3–1). These practice times include working individually, with a peer, and in small groups, and encompass math, science, and social studies as well as literature, reading, and writing. Since shared reading is my most important teaching time, I schedule it early in the school day after the children have settled in. We usually spend about forty-five minutes at this initial session, and then return to the rug area for shorter shared reading times throughout the day. (See Figures 3–2 and 3–3, which provide sample schedules for kindergarten and first- and second-grade classrooms.)

Guidelines for Planning

Since I believe that shared reading is an essential component of a reading/writing classroom, I plan carefully for each session. This doesn't mean that I outline every skill, strategy, and text in advance of a session, or that everything that I plan is carried out; I am always open to the interests of the students and direction that they might

Elements of a balanced reading program:

- Reading aloud
- Shared reading
- Silent reading
- Paired reading
- Guided reading
- Literature circles
- Response journals
- Book sharing
- One-on-one reading with the teacher
- Writing workshop

Figure 3–1   A Balanced Reading Program

lead us. Shared reading includes a combination of the interests, intentions, and goals of both the teacher and students, not unlike parent and child during a bedtime story. My plans must be well thought out, but flexible.

When working with beginning readers I use many texts that offer simple stories in very large print. As the children become independent readers and writers, I expose them to more complicated stories, sentence structure, and vocabulary. I want to match the shared reading texts with the students' current and near-future reading and writing development.

I include a variety of genres and texts with different word counts, sizes, fonts, and placement on the page. I present familiar songs, poems, and stories, and I introduce new ones. I also keep in mind the interests of the students, as well as the social studies and science themes that we are studying as a class (see Figure 3–4).

At the beginning of the year I find songs that the children know so that they feel comfortable and included in the classroom community that we are building. Along with these I add new texts,

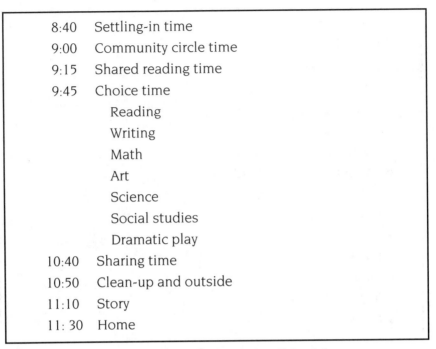

Figure 3–2 Sample Half-Day Kindergarten Schedule

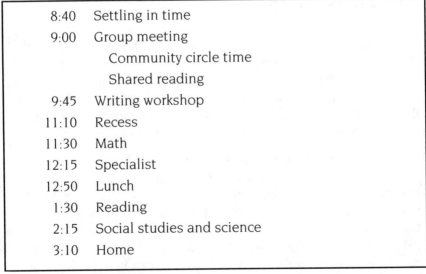

Figure 3–3 Sample Full-Day First- or Second-Grade Schedule

- Actions texts
- Biographies
- Body awareness texts
- Chants
- Counting texts
- Finger plays
- Informational books
- Informational storybooks
- Musical instruments
- Name texts
- Nursery rhymes
- Poems
- Puppets
- Raps
- Rounds
- Songs
- Song storybooks

Figure 3–4 Variety of Texts

and the children contribute their favorites from home as well. As the year goes on, we enjoy these texts over and over again, and create what Holdaway (1979) called "a repetoire of familiar texts." Familiarity supports learning to read, independence in reading, fluency, comprehension, and vocabulary development. Familiarity also supports love of learning. (See Figure 3–5.)

General Shared Reading Schedule

I always start shared reading with a song. Usually we sing several familiar songs, and sometimes I introduce a new one. Most are written on charts and hang from hangers from my teaching easel, but some are in big book form, such as *Bear Facts* (Gentner), *The Circus Is in Town* (Belanger), *Down by the Bay* (Daniel), and *Old MacDonald Had a Farm* (Daniel). During this warm-up or introduction time, we

Familiarity supports:

- learning to read
- independence in reading
- fluency
- comprehension
- vocabulary development
- love of learning

Figure 3–5 Familiarity

also read poems from charts and big books, such as from *Jewels* (Harwayne) and *Catch Me the Moon Daddy* (Kaufman). With both songs and poems we might stop to talk about what the text means, discuss something we notice about the print, explore a phonetic element, examine vocabulary in the context of the text, look at the pictures, and create a dance or act out the song.

Next we read two or three familiar big books. These are books the children ask for, ones the leader has selected, ones that go along with a current social studies or science theme, or books that have clear examples of a convention of print or phonetic element that I want to reinforce or introduce. If I have recently introduced a new big book, we reread it daily for about a week, so the children became familiar with it. They also practice it independently throughout the day (see Figure 3–6).

If I am going to introduce a new big book, I do so early into the session, after we have sung a few songs, because I know that reading a new big book takes time and I want the children to be alert and eager to participate. For example, before reading a storybook we predict what the book is about, and as we read we continue to predict what will happen next. Sometimes I put Post-its on certain words so we can explore vocabulary and look at the graphophonic elements in the texts. At the end of the session we read the story again without stopping. When I introduce an informational book, we spend time skimming the text, looking at the illustrations and photographs, and exploring the table of contents and index.

1. Warm-ups: three or four songs and a couple of poems.
2. Read several familiar big books or introduce a new big book.
3. End with a picture trade book.

Figure 3–6 Shared Reading Schedule

Picture Storybooks

Pre-school and elementary teachers have always read picture story-books to their students. I remember being told by my teacher that she would read to us at the end of the day, "if you are good, and if you finish all your work." I presume that the main purpose of this special reading time was to reward us for a day's work and to relax everyone before dismissal. Nowadays teachers are more aware of the pedagogical reasons for reading to their students, plan carefully what they will read, and are diligent to include reading aloud throughout the day. Aside from reading books that entertain and give joy, they select stories that pose problems, offer resolutions, teach about the world, provide models for writing, and help children understand how print works. (See Figure 3–7.)

Supportive Texts for Beginning Readers

In selecting big books and planning shared reading lessons for beginning readers, I choose some books that control the amount of

Picture storybooks

- entertain
- give joy
- pose problems
- offer resolutions
- teach about the world
- show how print works
- provide models for writing

Figure 3–7 The Value of Picture Storybooks

print on the page and the location of the print. When young readers read these books over and over again during shared reading and practice time, they memorize the text. When they are ready they begin to read word for word, matching each word with their voice and eye, with their memory of the text supporting them. One way to assess this word-voice match is to ask them to use a pointer as they read. Follow-up book projects during practice time encourages them to read the story again and again and think deeply about its meaning.

These simple texts can also be used to introduce and reinforce conventions of writing, such as punctuation, and teach parts of speech and extend vocabulary with independent readers. I suggest that teachers borrow big books from the earlier grades and use them in mini-lessons before writing workshop.

In a Dark, Dark Wood (Cowley and Melser) supports beginning readers who are learning to point word for word. It has five words on each page, all of which are written toward the bottom underneath the picture. The text is repetitive, with small variations reinforced by the illustrations. The letters are in large boldfaced type, and there is significant space between each word. After my kindergarteners have read it again and again, I give them the pointer and listen and watch how they read. They then make a pop-up book as a follow-up project (Fisher 1998).

The text pattern in the big book *The Queen Made a Quilt* (Rohman) is predictable, and its changes are supported by the colorful pictures. The six-word sentences on each page tell about a different colored quilt that the queen made. The quilt is described by an adjective and color word, such as, "She [the queen] made a thin, red quilt." Beginning readers can practice their reading with this text. I also use it with second graders to introduce adjectives and the place of the comma between two adjectives. The students can then draw their own quilts and write their own descriptions to go along with it.

Itch! Itch! (Blanchard and Suhr) repeats the same two lines on each page. Each picture shows someone scratching him- or herself because of poison ivy. A speech bubble (for example, "Oh, oh, my hand!") emphasizes a particular body part. I use the speech bubbles in this book to introduce direct quotations and quotations marks. First we read the bubbles together as part of the text. After the students are familiar with the book, I assign different children a page, and when we come to their part, they each stand up, recite their line, and act out their page by itching the body part mentioned. Teachers in higher grades can extend this activity by asking their students to write an innovation on the text using quotation marks instead of speech bubbles.

Introducing a Picture Storybook Big Book

I give a great deal of thought concerning how I will introduce a big book. First of all, I make certain that we will have at least half an hour to explore the book during its first reading. Much of our discussion involves prediction. We predict before we even see the book, and then again as we look at the cover. We predict throughout the reading, and at the end of the reading we predict possible sequels. Finally, we confirm or change our initial predictions. Whenever I spend too much time predicting, one of my students rescues us from my over-teaching by saying, "Let's just read the story." (See Figure 3–8.)

When I introduce a big book, we usually talk about the title before we look at the cover. For example, when I introduce *Crunchy Munchy* (Parkes) to a first-grade class, I write the title on the board and ask the students to tell what that phrase reminds them of and what they think the book might be about. My purpose is to help them activate their prior knowledge and expand this knowledge as they think about the book. As Margaret Moustafa (1997) suggests, "The amount of background knowledge children have on a topic prior to reading a passage has a powerful effect on their abilities to make sense of the passage" (64).

We can predict:

- before we see the book
- while we look at the cover
- throughout the reading
- at the end of the reading

Figure 3–8 Predicting Opportunities

Many of the students' responses usually have to do with food. Next, we look specifically at each word and make a list of things that are crunchy, such as candy, corn, and apples, and food that is munchy. We talk about how we munch on food that we like. When I show them the colorful cover, with a branch of apples, a pasture gate, and a cow, horse, goat, and pig, the children often point out that they have mentioned apples and that this is a farm story.

The simple story in *Crunchy Munchy* is reinforced by colorful illustrations that relate directly to the text. There are between two and six lines on each page, and *pig, goat, cow, horse,* and *apples* are the most prominent high-frequency print words in the text. I trust that through their repeated use, the children will learn to recognize them in the context of the story, and as they year goes on they begin to notice them in other stories and to use them in own their writing. The phrase "CRUNCHY MUNCHY, CRUNCHY MUNCHY," repeated throughout the story, provides the students with easy access to unison reading and helps them make analogies with other similar print words, such as *crumb, punchy,* and *lunch.* "As children learn to recognize more and more print words in context, their natural ability to make analogies between familiar and unfamiliar print words will help them figure out how to pronounce unfamiliar print words by themselves" (Moustafa 1997, 55).

For the first reading, I place Post-its on selected words throughout the text, and as we read we predict what the covered word might be. For example, with the sentence "They thought the apples would be sweet and juicy," I cover the word *juicy* and we make a list of possibilities. We discuss whether our choices make sense as part of the story and sound right in the sentence. Through this activity the students expand their vocabulary and learn that authors have choices in writing.

Since during this first reading we stop frequently to predict and discuss, in one respect we have interrupted the flow of the author's words and ideas. Therefore, before we end the session, I reread the story without stopping. But first I ask the children to share something they have noticed in the first reading that they are going to look for in the next reading. Examples often include, "I'm going to see if there are any other animals," "I'm going to count the apples," and "I want to see if the animals really get sick." These contributions, which tell what the students are noticing and interested in, are a means of sharing and teaching among peers, and a form of assessment for me.

Storybook Plan: *The Scrubbing Machine*

Sometimes I introduce a book by filling in a storybook plan with the class before the first reading, using only the information from the cover (Fisher 1995). I write the title while the children spell it out loud to me, which gives them practice with letter recognition and oral spelling. If they know Mrs. Wishy-Washy from previous books, they unanimously agree that she should be listed as the character (see Appendix A–1).

In one kindergarten we had a lively discussion about the place and time of the story. Since the picture on the cover didn't provide much information, the children agreed that it would make sense to write "in the house" for the place and "during the day" for the time, since that's where and when most people vacuum. Using prior knowledge from the original story of Mrs. Wishy-Washy, they decided that the mood of Mrs. Wishy-Washy would probably be angry.

After we read the story we went back to our original plan and made additions and corrections. One student was adamant that we include the scrubbing machine as a character since it seemed to be alive and have a mind of its own. Several children wanted to add cow, pig, and duck to the list of characters. Even though these animals only appear on two of the pages, the children had remembered them as important characters in the other story. We added "outside" and "in the shop" to the line for place, but we didn't change the time line (Figure 3–9).

The students provided many additions to their understanding of the mood of the story, and I used their spontaneous contributions as an opportunity to discuss and expand vocabulary. We took the role of Mrs. Wishy-Washy and read her comment to the shopkeeper—"This scrubbing machine just will not stop!"—using our different mood words: *angry, surprised, confused, sad,* and *frustrated.* We discussed how expression (intonation) adds to meaning when we read.

Learning Letters and Sounds and Unfamiliar Print Words

Shared reading provides continuous and various ways to help children learn letters and sounds and to pronounce or read unfamiliar

Name_____Date_____

STORYBOOK PLAN

TITLE The Scrubbing Machine

CHARACTERS Mrs. Wishy Washy / cow
                                    pig
                                    duck
                                    scrubbing
                                    machine

PLACE in the house / outside
                       in the shop

TIME during the day

MOOD angry / surprised
               confused
               sad
               frustrated

Figure 3-9 Storybook Plan

print words. Many kindergarten teachers tell me that they teach more about letters and phonological awareness in shared reading than they did when they were teaching with a letter-of-the-week program (Fisher 1998). When we teach in context, children understand how letters and sounds are used in authentic reading and writing, and they get to practice in meaningful contexts.

Letter recognition permeates shared reading in primary classrooms. When I work with pre-kindergarten or kindergarten children, we talk a great deal about the letters and sounds in the texts we are reading because I know that children in those grades are learning print knowledge. When I work with second graders, we concentrate on vocabulary and sentence structure they are likely to meet in their reading and writing.

Often the children are familiar with many of the words that they *hear* in a story and are ready to recognize them in print form. During shared reading teachers can reinforce this strategy to help children read and spell more and more words. For example, in the rhyming story *This Is the Bear* (Hayes), children can easily read along and predict what the final word in the line will be. In a class where I was a visiting teacher, I put Post-its on the word as a way to focus on the onset or rime, and we worked on the word *back* in the following sentence.

> *This is the man who picked up the sack.*
> *This is the driver who would not come back.*

I covered the entire word and we predicted what it could be. Then we confirmed our answer. Typically, the children came up with the word *back*. Then I said, "If it's *back*, what will the word begin with? What will it end with? If we can spell *sack*, how will we spell *back*?" This discussion initiated a list of the word families for /ack/, which the classroom teacher planned to add to throughout the year as the class came across other words that fit the list. During practice time, the children would use these lists in their writing. I also leave the Post-its in the book so the children can use them in their own way during practice time.

When children study words in the context of a book, they learn that all rhyming words are not spelled exactly the same, and that sometimes authors use words that only approximate a rhyme. In this story, when we came to *bus* and *fuss*, and *cross* and *lost*, we discussed the variations in spelling.

The following sentence introduced a discussion about author choice.

This is the bear who went to the dump,
And fell on the pile with a bit of a bump.

I covered the word *bump*, and we made a list of all the words that would make sense and sound right in its place. For example, the children came up with *clump*, *bump*, *jump*, and *thump*. After we checked the word that the author chose, we looked at our list. I asked, "If you were the author, which word would you have used?" I wanted them to understand that authors, including themselves, have choices.

This book provides many other teaching and learning possibilities. Aside from the story told in the text, there is another story told in the pictures, which the children can tell about either orally or in writing. The ending suggests that another episode is beginning, and they can talk and write about what that could be. Also,the speech bubbles provide an introduction to direct quotations and quotation marks.

Jolly Olly (Plater) is a rhyming poetry storybook that provides opportunities for children to work with letter recognition, onsets and rimes, and vocabulary. I use this book with kindergarten classes in which some of the students are just beginning to learn some letters, while others are beginning to read. There are learning possibilities for everyone. For example, in the following sentence, we focus on uppercase letters for names, the letter F, the onsets L (one consonant) and *fl* (consonant blend), the rimes *ute* and *olly*, the meaning of the word *lute*, and punctuation marks (comma, period, ellipses):

Jolly Olly buys a FLUTE,
But the F drops off.
He drives away with a merry . . .
LUTE.

Informational Books

When I first started teaching I primarily read picture books to my classes. Over the years, however, I realized that young children are extremely interested in the world about them, and that many would rather spend time with science or social studies books than with a storybook. In fact, in my kindergarten and first-grade classrooms over the years, I had many children who learned to read primarily through nonfiction. In *Thinking and Learning Together* (Fisher 1995) I discuss informational books and informational storybooks separately, but in this chapter I have grouped them together. Both informational books and informational storybooks impart factual information, but informational storybooks present the information within a story line.

A variety of informational books provide our students with different means to learn about the world, and such books help them envision ways they can express themselves as writers (see Figure 3–10). The models we show during shared reading often become models for reports and projects.

Using a Table of Contents, Index, and Glossary
When I introduce a nonfiction big book, I show the class that I read an information book differently than a storybook, which I read from

---

Informational books help students learn about:

- The world
- Skimming for information
- Tables of contents
- Indices
- Glossaries
- Illustrations
- Photographs
- Diagrams

Figure 3–10 Informational Books

beginning to end. First we thumb through the book to see what it is about and to get a sense of the format. For example, we check to discover if there are any illustrations, photographs, or diagrams.

Next we read through the table of contents to see the main topics of the book. In subsequent readings we return to the contents and explore the index. Through the repeated use and investigation of a single text, we select different sections that we want to explore at the moment. Starting this general exploration of informational books in kindergarten helps the children begin to acquire research skills they will need as they move through the grades.

Our Eyes (Robinson) is one of three informational books in a series entitled "Eyes and Ears." After flipping through the book with a group of second graders I was visiting, we read the table of contents, and when I asked for suggestions about which chapter to read first, a girl with glasses asked for "Vision Problems," which we noted started on page 14. During this session we only read the first two pages of the section because the children had so much to share and discuss. I left the book for them to read during practice time throughout the day, and when I came to pick it up, they called me over and excitedly told me all they had discovered on their own.

The index in *Exploring Land Habitats* (Phinney) is extensive and includes many land animals that children know. One of my favorite ways to explore this index is to ask students to recall an animal that they saw when we first skimmed the book. If the animal is listed in the index, we turn to the page and talk about the ways that the author and illustrator chose to give the information about its habitat and survival cycle. For example, there is a two-part diagram of the survival cycle of the ground squirrel, showing the dry season and rainy season. At the bottom of the page is a cartoon with a speech bubble telling how hair can protect animals from the heat, and a picture of an Inca dove with a question asking the reader to find the bird on the previous page.

Using a glossary, which is like a mini-dictionary, is an excellent way to demonstrate dictionary skills and how to apply them strategically. In *Journey to the Sea: The Snake River* (Wilde), the glossary, which is on the same page as the index, lists in alphabetical order ten geographical terms that are important in understanding the text. This format provides a practical, flexible way for the class to discuss vocabulary in context. For example, we can start with the word in the text and then turn to the glossary definition, or we can start with the definition and discuss how it applies to the use of the word in the text.

Illustrations, Photographs, and Diagrams

During shared reading we can also explore dictionary skills through big book dictionaries and alphabet books. For example, *Picture Perfect Word Book* (Johnson) provides the word definitions through pictures, diagrams, and words. For *families*, there are pictures of family members labeled in a family tree. The adjectives and illustrations in the alphabet book *Debra's Dog* (McDonald) provide extensive opportunities to discuss alphabetical order and vocabulary in meaningful context.

The models we show during shared reading become models for reports and projects, and the illustrations, photographs, and diagrams are important learning tools in this process. *Tadpole Diary* (Drew) includes photographs and diagrams to teach about the life cycle of a frog. In diary format it shows the transformation from egg to frog. One teacher used this book over a sixteen-week period with her first graders as they observed the cycle from egg to tadpoles to frogs in their classroom. They used the book as a guide to keep their tadpoles alive, as a manual for learning about tadpoles and frogs, and as a model for making their own tadpole diaries.

In *Hiking in the* U.S.A. (Traynor), the illustrations, which depict different geographical locations in the United States, support the poetic text. Each poem includes a rich, expressive adjective and noun portraying the landmark on the full-spread page. For example, the Gateway Arch in St. Louis is described as "glimmering" and "rising above me." During shared reading a class might discuss the author's vocabulary choices and then talk about alternative words they might use. Then during practice time the students can create their own extensions as they research places to write about.

Chickens (Snowball) is an information book that beginning readers can learn to read. In simple language, supported by illustrations and diagrams, it tells the life cycle of a chicken. Over several pages the reader is asked if the chickens are ready to hatch, and the answer is given in pop-up form, with the answer, accompanied by a diagram of the embryo, under the lift-up eggshell.

Planning and carrying out shared reading time in my classroom includes the following: scheduling shared reading for the same time each day, and being sure to plan enough time (thirty to forty-five minutes); reading a variety of texts in a variety of ways; using texts that students and I like, as well as texts that are part of the curriculum; including the skills and strategies that I notice my students are working on in their independent reading and writing (as well as those included in school or state standards and testing); and keeping the sessions joyful, remembering that students learn best in a caring learning community.

> *The unison situation, properly controlled in a lively and meaningful spirit, allows for massive individual practice by every pupil in the teaching context.*
> *(Holdaway 1979, 129)*

Part Two

Perspectives of a First-Year Teacher

4

Preparation and Materials

As I write this chapter, I am completing my first year of teaching. My master's degree thesis was on shared reading. My goal was to determine how effectively I could use the model to teach the skills and strategies of reading, while creating a foundation for loving reading and learning.

I began to prepare for shared reading by selecting and collecting the supplies and equipment I thought I would need. In order to create an atmosphere that would encourage and foster the components of Holdaway's (1979) Natural Classroom Learning Model, *demonstration, participation, practice,* and *performance,* I planned for specific conditions and materials for the room. This chapter is divided into three parts. The first focuses on setting up the shared reading area in the room. The second details the materials that I have found most useful in shared reading, and the third part addresses the types of texts that I use.

Setting Up the Shared Reading Area

Rug Area

Based on the model of the bedtime story, shared reading should take place in a compact and close area. The students sit where they can comfortably see the texts and each other, ideally on a rug. This area becomes the space for group demonstration and participation and is associated with enjoyment and positive experiences. I usually sit on a stool at the edge of the rug by the easel and whiteboard. I keep my big books, charts, and basket of supplies near my stool (see Figure 4–1).

Easel and Book Board

In the rug area, I have an easel with a book board. I store other materials and supplies used for shared reading close to the easel so I can easily access what I need on a given day. The easel provides a resting place for big books and frees my hands to write, point, mask, or move around. A book board is helpful because it is sturdy, keeping the books upright. However, a strong easel that is high enough so all students can clearly see the texts is sufficient. When I use an easel to hold big books, students can approach the text and turn pages independently when they are highlighting a part of the text. Because I am not controlling the book, I become more of a member of the group, rather than the authority of the texts.

Whiteboard (or Chalkboard)

Writing, looking at letters and words, and creating word lists is an integral part of shared reading. I have a whiteboard accessible and

---

Supply basket contents:

- pointers
- Post-it notes
- pens and markers
- masks of different sizes
- highlighter tape
- cut flyswatter
- sliding ruler
- Wicky Stix
- whiteboard, markers, and eraser
- puppets and role tags
- students name tags
- scrap paper with envelopes for sorting words
- notebook to jot notes to myself about a topic or student

Figure 4–1 The Supply Basket

visible during each session. Another easel with large paper or a portable writing board could also be used for the many times writing occurs. As students offer questions, comments, or other insights, I use the board to connect the oral with the visual. We create lists, compare interesting spelling patterns, and talk about letter formation.

One day, I used the whiteboard after reading a poem during shared reading. Marcus shared that *do* and *you* rhyme but do not have the same ending. We explored other words that rhyme with *do* and *you* (*true, new, too, two*) and noticed that many of the endings were different. This interested students; they had been accustomed to words rhyming only if they had the same ending. The students brainstormed other words that rhyme with *do*, and I wrote them on a large piece of paper as we talked about the letters and sounds of each word. We cut the paper, categorized the words according to their endings, and taped the words onto a new piece of paper. I kept the word lists so we could add to them as we found more rhymes in other texts.

Chart Storage and Hangers
Charts that are left rolled up are hard to locate, cumbersome to work with, and therefore not used. Attaching charts to regular wire clothes hangers makes storage and use easy and efficient. I attach one chart to each side of a single hanger. I use clear packing tape to secure the back of the first chart to the hanger, leaving the hanger loop above the chart. I tape the top of the second chart to the top of the first, again leaving a space for the loop (Figure 4–2). I can then hang the chart with either side facing the group. I store the charts by hanging them across the blackboard top and on hooks in the wall. They could also be stored in a closet or portable stand, as long as the students have full and independent access to them throughout the day.

Materials

Masks
I got the idea of masks and masking questions from my mother. I make masks of various sizes out of stiff, black tagboard or thick, white Styrofoam. I have different masks for individual letters, punctuation,

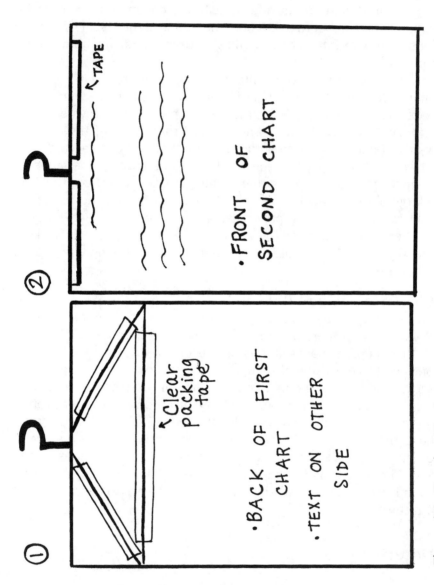

Figure 4-2 Hanging Charts

and short, medium, and long words. Since many big books are published with different fonts and print sizes, I create specific masks to fit each book. I also make masks that fit my charts and other enlarged texts. Then, when children come to the chart to mask a word, they also select which size mask they believe will best fit the word (see patterns for masks Appendix A–2).

Through a variety of masking questions, I can quickly assess whether a student is familiar with the concepts of letters and word lengths. (See Figure 4–3.) For example, I'll know that Jeremy needs some more discussion of what a letter is if he chooses the largest mask, which fits a seven-letter word, to mask the single letter J.

Who would like to come and mask . . .

- a letter you know?
- a word you know?
- the letter your first (last) name begins with?
- a letter in your name?
- your favorite letter?
- the letter that begins your friend's name?
- the letter _____?
- the letter with the sound _____?
- the letter before _____?
- the letter after _____?
- the letter between _____ and _____?
- a lowercase _____?
- an uppercase _____?
- a short word?
- a medium-sized word?
- a long word?
- a word with one (two, three . . .) letters?

Figure 4–3 Masking Questions for Conventions of Print
(continues on p. 50)

Adapted from *Joyful Learning in Kindergarten, Revised Edition* by
Bobbi Fisher

- a word that begins with _____?
- a word that ends with _____?
- a word with the blend _____?
- the word _____?
- a word that means about the same as _____?
- a word that means the opposite of _____?
- a compound word?
- a color word?
- an action word?
- the name of a person, place, or thing?
- a word with the ending -ing (-ly, -ed . . .)?
- a period (question mark, quotation marks . . .)?
- the contraction for _____?
- the first word on the page we are going to read?
- the last word on the page we are going to read?

Others

- a word that is plural?
- a word that rhymes with _____?
- a word that ends with the letter between _____ and _____?

Figure 4–3 Continued

Other Masking Tools

A *flyswatter* with a rectangle cut out of the center allows students to hold it and stand farther away from the text. It does not, however, block out the surrounding text as well as a dark mask.

Wicky Stix are colorful, pliable strings of wax sold in teacher stores. They are used to underline words, circle letters, divide parts of words, or highlight specific areas of a text. My students enjoy using Wicky Stix because the strings remain on the text and are referred to throughout the shared reading discussion.

Highlighter tape works well to accent certain words, letters, punctuation marks, or other aspects of the text. It is removable and available at office supply stores.

The masking tools not only bring the children physically to the book and enable them to be active participants, but they also help focus the class on the specific details of print. There is no doubt about what letter, word, or piece we are discussing.

Pointers

Pointing to each word on the enlarged text reiterates the notion that there is a one-to-one correspondence between the word on the page and the word we read. Students discover that meaning is derived from the printed text and that the text remains constant; the same story is read each time that the book is read. Holdaway (1979) encourages the use of pointing during shared reading in order to guide students to learn that print is read from left to right and then begins back at the left as it works down the page.

I use long dowels or rulers to point to the words as we read. I also have some fancier pointers: sticks with shapes, sticks with streamers, and sticks of several different lengths. Students often pick up the pointers during workshop time and read big books, charts, and other texts and words in the room while pointing.

Post-its

I use Post-its to cover words ahead of time to generate prediction and discussion. One dark Post-it will sufficiently cover most text; the lighter, pastel colors usually require two. (If a student does read through the Post-it, I know she is paying attention and engaging in a clever way of confirming the "hidden text.")

Using Post-its and masks in meaningful texts helps my students understand the complexity of spelling, grammar, vocabulary, and other literacy conventions (Figure 4–4). As we read together, we look at exceptions and anomalies as well as patterns. Students can better understand the complexities of language if they are aware it's not just a series of rules.

Discussion Questions

Have we seen this word before?

Does that make sense?

Does it sound right to you?

What letters would we expect if it is _____?

How else could we spell that word?

How do you think they spell it in books?

What can you do to find out what this word is?

If this word is _____, how do you think it would end?

Let's listen to that word. What letter would you expect to see in the middle . . . after the *x* . . . before the *-ing*?

Count the letters in this word.

Count the words in this line.

What makes you think it will be _____?

How sure can we be that this is_____?

What more do we need to know to be sure of this word?

If this word is _____, what letter would we expect to see here?

How can we find the *two* or *hippopotamus*?

Why are they different in length?

Figure 4–4 Questions for Discussion
Adapted from *Foundations of Literacy* by Don Holdaway

During shared reading, the group may generate long lists of possibilities for a covered word. We then peek at the first letter, re-assess our predictions, and make new ones. We use the cueing systems (Figure 2–4) in our predictions: Does our choice make sense in the sentence and story (semantic)? Does it sound right (syntactic)? Does it look right (grapho-phonemic)?

One evening before school, I took *The Three Little Pigs* (Parkes), a book with a lot of dialogue, and used Post-its to cover each word that indicated someone was talking (e.g., *said, shouted, cried,* etc.). As we read the book together, we brainstormed possible synonyms for each covered word, and the class chose which one to put on each particular Post-it.

This experience allowed us to quickly address the cueing systems. As we worked through how to write each word on the Post-it, we had to discuss the sounds, letters, and spelling patterns (graphophonics) of each word. For example, when the word we picked was *yelled*, we discussed the sounds of the word and noticed that *yelled* was spelled and sounded like the word *yellow*.

We addressed syntax and determined that the missing word needed to be a verb. We also noticed that in this story the verbs were in the past tense. Here, I briefly addressed the concept of root or base words and endings. When we had made our selection, I asked the class, "Does it sound right when we read back our choices?"

Semantics came into play when we looked at the meanings of the words we selected. When the illustration showed an angry character with a red face, we agreed that while *whispered* would sound right, it would not make sense for the meaning of the story.

We reread our rendition and then compared it to the author's version. We talked about the choices that authors have and concluded that it is far more interesting and descriptive to use different words in writing than to simply always write *said* when someone speaks.

Name Tags

While most of the participation in shared reading occurs as a group, throughout the sessions there are opportunities for individual students to come up and mask, choose the next poem, or play a role in readers theater. Very quickly, it becomes too time- and energy-consuming for teachers to remember who was last called on. The students however, do keep track and are adamant about fairness. Consequently, I create a name tag for each student, using only first names. I show the group all of the tags and explain that when a name is drawn from the pile, it will be moved to another pile. After the first pile is done, I shuffle the tags and begin again. I want the students to know that the system is fair and that everyone will eventually have a turn.

I also like name tags for the literacy mini-lessons they initiate. Sometimes when I pick a name from the pile I show it to the class so they can read it. Often they remember who has and has not yet been picked that round, so before looking they find it exciting to guess what name could be next. From time to time I cover all but the first or last letter of a name and the students predict whose tag it is. The students often choose to write about their friends and use the tags to help them spell their names.

For example, an unanticipated mini-lesson occurred when a student was convinced that I had arranged the name tags in alphabetical order. His name was near the end of the alphabet, so he was disturbed. As he was focusing completely on the order of the tags, I decided to take a minute to explore his idea. We looked at the previously selected tags (Marcus and Molly). I asked the group where the current pick (Maggie) fit alphabetically. One child in the group knew to look beyond the first two letters. "No! Maggie should be before Marcus!"

The group then decided to arrange the name tags in alphabetical order on a table. The names Marcus and Maggie required looking at the third letter. Then they they put in Molly. I did not give a rule for how to put them in order. Instead, some students figured it out on their own and others learned from them. They were probably engaged in this activity because, as Holdaway (1979) asserts, names are "highly meaningful personal words" (114).

The students were invested in this activity; they wanted to know where they stood alphabetically in the group. I had not planned to talk about third-place alphabetizing, but I went with the group's eagerness and took a few minutes to explore a concept that they were interested in investigating. I did not define a rule and require them to apply it; I simply offered the time and support for them to problem solve. As Holdaway has noted, "our definition of teaching needs to move over towards inducing individual learners into mindful action rather than providing them with a pre-packed kit of rules" (99).

Puppets

Using puppets in a readers theater or for role-playing allows students not only to physically move about but also to dramatize and become a character. I get a clearer overall sense of each student by observing his or her acting and role-playing.

My mom gave me the idea of generic puppets. They are made out of plain fabric and have two arms and a head (see pattern in Appendix A–3). They are simple so they can be given a variety of roles. The focus is not on which puppet is the best, but rather the roles and texts we are using. For readers theater, the students stand up in front of the group, and no puppet theater is necessary. I select the roles for the students by picking name tags.

Role Tags

I keep clear plastic name tag holders and blank index cards near the rug area in order to make tags to identify actors' roles. Some big books and poems also lend themselves to drama, not simply books in play form. For example, when we were acting out *The Three Little Pigs*, I wrote the names of the characters on index cards and put them in the plastic holders. Children representing the different characters wore them as we read the story at readers theater.

Texts

Song, Poems, and Chant Charts

Charts are an important component of shared reading. I use large (27″ × 34″), heavy, lined chart paper from office supply stores. The heavier stock is a little more expensive, but the charts last longer than regular paper. It is best to use thick, black markers to write the words; the dark ink helps everyone see the text. In order for the words to be clear, make letters one to two inches high. I use colored markers to draw identifying pictures and highlight specific words.

When I create charts I choose songs, poems, and chants that I enjoy and that span a variety of genres. I try to include poems of different types (rhymes, free verse, couplets) and topics (funny, serious). It does not take long to build a large collection simply by reading through poetry and songbooks. I do not look for texts that serve specific lesson purposes because I believe that with a wide enough variety of interesting, pleasing, and stimulating material, there will be sufficient language experiences to address and discuss. The focus is on the meaning of the text.

Once I introduce the charts, I leave them out in the classroom so students can easily locate specific texts and use them independently during workshop and throughout the day. Though it is time-consuming to create charts, it is time well spent. One chart may be read repeatedly in shared reading, used by students to practice their new skills and reading throughout the day, and referred to during student performance.

Big Books

I use big books from different publishers. I use fiction, nonfiction, plays, and poetry to introduce many concepts in meaningful and relevant ways. It is also beneficial to have the same books available in standard size for students to take home and read independently.

As with the charts, the big books are accessible to all students throughout the day. I hang the big books on the rungs of a wooden clothes dryer. This enables the children to find the specific titles they want to read, and it lets them replace the books without help.

Many students read the big books alone, in pairs, or with a group of friends as they practice their maturing literacy. I keep the pointers and masks near the big books so students can engage in independent forms of shared reading.

Poem Pieces

I write each word of a short poem on an individual card and place the cards in a labeled envelope with a copy of the full text. After we share the poem during shared reading, I show the cards to the group and invite them to "make the poem" by laying the cards out in the correct order. Sometimes two or three students randomly divide up the cards and make the poem together. They also enjoy rearranging the cards to create new sentences. As they manipulate the words, they experience a type of editing. When they read a new version that does not make sense, they learn that some aspects of writing are negotiable while others are not.

One of the poems that we read and recited many times was "Peanut Butter":

> A peanut sat down on a railroad track,
> His heart was all a-flutter.
> The five-fifteen came rushing by,
> Toot! Toot!
> Peanut butter!

I then offered the poem pieces to the group. The children discussed the pieces together: "We each have the same word [peanut], but mine has to go now because yours has a capital letter."

"Why?"

"Because your card starts the line. Look [at the original text]. It is the beginning of the sentence."

"Hey, *railroad* is a compound word!"

"We both have *Toot!* but they are exactly the same so it doesn't matter whose goes first."

Class Songbook

I type each song that we learn and create two copies of a class songbook. The songs are on individual pages and bound in three-ring binders. Students are encouraged to illustrate the books. The drawings help some students quickly identify which song is on the page. Most students are successful singers independently because we have sung the songs many times together. The students also make their own songbooks by copying and illustrating the songs.

Songbooks and Music Tapes

Occasionally, we sing along with the tapes during shared reading. Some of the tapes have a narrated story to accompany the song. If I do not have access to the tape, usually the score is included in the book, so I learn the tune with help from a keyboard or the music teacher. Music involves the students in an alternate sign system and eases their familiarity with the lyrics. I often hear our songs sung throughout the day. I leave the tapes and books at the listening center for students to choose during follow-up time.

5

Methods and Strategies

Getting Started

During the summer I started collecting big books and creating a variety of charts. Although I knew I would need to have songs, poems, chants, and texts that are interesting and encourage discussion, I did not know how many texts I would have time for in a session, so I made as many charts as I could and tried to have a wide variety of lengths and topics (see Figure 5–1).

The First Day

On the first day of school I used one songbook, one big book, three poems, and two songs on charts. I also had a trade book for an ending read aloud. I arranged the rug area with an easel and access to a whiteboard. I kept all of my supplies for shared reading in a basket near my chair, knowing that organization and immediate access to supplies is important to a successful session.

At the beginning of the year, I started with songs that were familiar to the students because children enjoy singing songs they know. These songs also increased their comfort and confidence levels. On my first day, I began by singing *Baby Beluga* while pointing to each word on the chart. Most students quickly caught on that they should come to the rug area. I motioned to those who weren't sure. By the end of the song, I had everyone there. Since this activity was new to the students, I took a few minutes to explain my two expectations when I start to sing each day: (1) they need to be part of the

Do I have poems and song . . .

> of different lengths?
>
> that rhyme?
>
> that don't rhyme?
>
> that are seasonal or specific to months, days, holidays?
>
> that are related to content that the children would enjoy?
>
> that are related to content area that are required by my school's standards?
>
> that are serious?
>
> that are silly and funny?
>
> that are written by a variety of authors (male and female, adult and children, different backgrounds and ethnicity)?

Figure 5–1   Things to Keep in Mind When Making Charts

group when the song is over; and (2) everyone has to be quiet when the song ends so we can move on to discussions and other texts.

Keeping Track

I devised a planning form in order to keep track of the texts I use as well as the skills and strategies that I plan to address. After each session, I add to the form any discussions or concepts that we covered in shared reading that I had not anticipated. I also add notes about specific texts, such as which books, poems, or songs the students requested, what skills and/or strategies were reiterated, what kind of content discussion took place (Figure 5–2). The form is useful for me because I want to be organized about what we are accomplishing without designing a strict, prescriptive agenda. I keep each week's form in a notebook for easy reference. (A blank form appears as Appendix A–4.)

Creating a Schedule

In a typical shared reading session, I begin with a "gathering" song. After the class is ready at the rug, we continue with another song and a short poem for warm-ups. Following our warm-up material, I

	Monday	Tuesday	Wednesday	Thursday	Friday
Warm Ups: song poem chant	song: Hey Cadi poem: Toot Toot	song: Busy Bees poem: Birthday	song: Predator poem: Who has seen the Wind?	song: Busy Bees poem: Top of Hill	song: Predator poem: Rain (→)
New:	Meet the Octopus	(Busy Bees)	(Toot Toot) .sticky way	Three Billy Goats Gruff theater	(→) poem
Type:	nonfiction	song			
Other/Old	Letter from Miss Compassion . letter format	Meet the Octopus . write to Miss C.	Meet the Octopus	Birthday poem	Three Billy Goats Gruff
Focus + Skills	. nonfiction - don't have to read front to back . observations - What do you notice? . table of contents . index . ABC order (who would you use?) = initial consonant	. months (meaning) . rhyming words . L. Read: oi ay (table of contents & meeting in section . labels)	. locating information . headings & captions . armoire - looking at something small	. dialogue & sentence phrasing . roles → tags = oi oy	. continue readers theater = compound words butcher paper
Notes		- Diagrams	- song tape for Busy Bees	introduce poem pieces	
Read Aloud	Jimmy's Boa	Sylvester	Chrysanthemum	Amelia Bedelia	Mouse Mouse

Figure 5-2 Planning Form

introduce a new big book or chart. We spend the bulk of our shared reading time on this main text. We end our session by rereading and discussing a previously introduced book or chart. Finally, I read aloud a trade book (see Figure 5–3).

Texts

Texts for shared reading can include a variety of forms. I generally use homemade charts of short stories, poems, or songs and big books. Other texts that are large enough for the class to see and read can be used as well, such as small predictable books, trade books, posters, newspaper headlines, advertisements, and large student work.

Songs

We always begin with a song, either from a chart or an enlarged songbook. Singing gives the students time to finish a conversation or complete a task they are working on before joining the group. I know that if a student is not present for the entire song, he or she will not miss a key lesson. Nor will students miss out on singing a particular song because we return to songs again and again. In calling the group together through singing, I do not have to yell or disrupt the tone of the day by interrupting in a controlling manner.

Before singing a new song, I become very familiar with the

Typical shared reading schedule:

- Gathering song
- Familiar song
- Short poem
- New text
- Big book
- Chart
- Familiar text
- Ending song
- Teacher read aloud

Figure 5–3 Typical Shared Reading Schedule

tune. Usually I listen to the tapes on my way to and from school. I also have a keyboard to jog my memory as I follow the score printed in the book.

The Predator (Gentner) is a rhyming song about a snake who gets closer and closer to his prey. The song begins softly and gradually gets louder and louder until it reaches the surprise ending. This song conveys a lot of information in a simple manner. Each page gives us one more fact about the snake. After enjoying the song for a few days, we made a list of all of the things we learned about snakes. One student contributed a fact for our list based on a picture.

I use *Munch, Munch, Munch* (Gentner) to incorporate some math mini-lessons. This book has a predictable text that takes the reader through the stages of the life cycle of a butterfly. Every few pages a key word in the story is repeated eight times. One day, I asked the students to count in their head the number of times *munch* was on a specific page. I instructed them to whisper their answer when I put my pointer down. After the class had whispered "eight," I asked for volunteers to explain to the class how they arrived at their answer. Their answers helped me assess their math reasoning. Some answers included: "I counted 1, 2, 3, 4, 5, 6, 7, 8." "I went 2, 4, 6, 8." "I counted 1, 2, 3, 4, 1, 2, 3, 4 and knew that four plus four is eight." "I just saw eight."

Other times, I interject questions such as "If the word *hide* is on this page eight times, how many times is the letter *h* on this page?" or "We found the word *sleep* eight times on this page. So, how many *e's* are on this page?"

I found that the big songbook *Frog on a Log* (Gentner) fit my curriculum on animal life cycles. The story relays the life cycle of a frog and teaches many facts and related vocabulary. It is a rhyming song and ends each line by spelling the word and giving the sign language symbol for each letter. We slow down to sign and sing. The signing makes us deliberately concentrate on the letters and words. After using this book, some children became interested in sign language and consequently learned how to sign their names.

Short Poems

I usually follow the song with a short poem. Short poems quickly become very familiar to the children, and they are soon able to read them alone. Sometimes I select several volunteers to come up and read short poems by themselves, which gives them a chance to read confidently in front of the class.

A favorite poem is "Apples, Peaches, Pears, and Plums." This poem asks the reader about his or her birthday and lists the months of the year in order. I draw several name tags and have the students come to the text and affix a Wicky Stix in a circle around the month of their birthday. For follow-up, students use my chart and poem pieces and re-create the poem next to the chart on the floor. This poem helps many children learn the sequence of the months of the year.

Familiar Texts

Following the songs, we reread a familiar text. Sometimes the students guess which book I have selected. I give them oral and written literacy clues, such as "Well, the first letter in the title is an O." As predictions are made I narrow the possibilities. For example, "The last letter in the first word of the title is D." Of course once the book *Old Black Fly* (Aylesworth) is revealed, we confirm my clues and read it together. Other times, I select a student's name from my name tag pile and ask that student to choose a previously read text to reread with the group.

Bringing back familiar texts serves several purposes: it involves student choice; it reiterates the constancy of print; it empowers the students through ownership and familiarity of texts; and it gives an opportunity for review of previously addressed concepts. Old texts also provide another opportunity to discover ideas about the text that were not addressed at the initial reading. I have also found that the students particularly enjoy returning to texts (see Figure 5–4).

Student Choice

I soon learned how important it is to listen to the students' choices when selecting texts to reread. During one session, I found that my assumptions about what the students liked and disliked were not accurate. The previous day we had read a couple of poems from a big book of poetry titled *Morning, Noon, and Night: Poems to Fill Your Day* (Taberski). "Pick Up Your Room" was somewhat difficult to read because it was written with figurative speech, and I didn't feel the whole group was involved. In fact, I had thought that the group

Familiar texts:

- involve student choice
- reiterate the constancy of print
- empower the students through ownership and confident reading
- give an opportunity for review of previously addressed concepts
- provide an opportunity to discover new ideas about the text
- bring enjoyment
- unify the classroom community

Figure 5–4 Familiar Texts

seemed bored with that poem. The following day, however, when I asked them what poem they would like to read from the anthology, they called for "Pick Up Your Room." They remembered it as amusing and mysterious. More students participated and more discussion about the words in the text followed the reading.

I learned from that experience that I am not the ultimate judge of what students like or do not like, or even what is too hard for them. Many things are difficult to learn on the first try. This experience highlighted to me the necessity for students to have multiple opportunities to read and practice and work with texts. I found that the students were finding new issues to discuss with each subsequent reading of the same poem or book. Student choice and the permission to reread were tied to the overall safe environment I had hoped to create.

Introducing and Using a New Fiction Text

There are various ways in which I introduce new books. Sometimes I begin by slowly writing the first letter of the new title on the board, and the children focus on letter shapes and rule out certain letters based on formation. Once the letter is identified, students guess what the word could be. The choices are narrowed as more letters are added until finally the word is revealed. Then I fill in the remainder of the title.

When everyone knows the title, I ask the students what the cover might look like and for predictions about the content. After several guesses as to what the book might be about, we look at the cover and make more informed predictions. We wonder who the characters are and why the illustrator designed the cover the way he or she did. We assess what kind of book we think it will be (e.g., funny, scary, sad, happy). We also talk about who might be in the story and where we think it will take place.

When I introduced *Goodnight, Goodnight* (Parkes), I placed Post-its over the last word in the couplets on each page in order to generate predictions about rhyming words. The students gave suggestions for possible words, and together we spelled the words on the Post-its. We read through the book again with our word choices and asked ourselves if it made sense and sounded right. Then we compared what we wrote with what the author chose. After this activity, I asked the students to share what they had noticed about the book.

Tyler commented on the unusual pictures in the book. The background was abstract, and he asked the other students what they thought the shapes and lines were. This discussion moved on to the role of the illustrator and the decisions that are involved in book illustrations. We located the illustrator's name on the cover and title page.

Molly located two compound words. She used the Wicky Stix to divide the words.

Marcus saw two contractions. As a class we wrote the contractions out as two words on Post-its and placed them over the original contractions in the text. Then we read the new sentences. On a poster we started a running list of contractions and the words they stand for, and as we noticed contractions in other books and songs, we added them to the list. We eventually grouped them according to *to be, not, have,* and *will* contractions.

Andrew commented that there were a lot of words with *ght*. We went back to find the first one and Andrew explained, "You see the *fi* in *fight*. You hear the *t*, but not the *gh*. That is silent. It is like *might, light, night.*" We generated a long list of the words, which I wrote on the whiteboard next to the easel.

Jeremy noticed that "to give a fright" was a funny way to say *frightened.* "It is like you are giving someone a fright, like a bad present." We noted that the author could have written *scared* but it would not have been as interesting and it would not have fit with her rhyming pattern. I expected the students would use these mini-lessons to think about word choice in their own writing.

I Notice

After I had established the routine of asking the children to share something they've noticed, students began looking more closely at texts. I was able to learn about each student's development based on what they noticed from day to day. Endless possibilities result from allowing students to contribute what they observe.

Jeannine noticed that three of our favorite songbooks were by the same author; Rebecca noticed that in *Munch, Munch, Munch* (Gentner) the author always repeated a word eight times after the phrase "To become such beautiful things"; Tyler showed us that the letter *j* in one particular book looked more like a long *i* due to the font; Andrew noticed the number of times that the word POP was in a poem; Karl shared a word that started with the same letter as his name; Marcus noticed that there were two contractions on the same page in *Goodnight, Goodnight* (Parkes); Molly noticed that *cheek* and *chin* both have *ch*; Greg had counted the number of times *and* was used in a poem and pointed out that all of the *ands* were right underneath each other; Maggie told us that she did not think the drawing for the poem "Cats" went with what the poem was about, and described how she would have drawn it differently; Chris shared that the words *Buzz, Buzz* in the big book *Busy Bees* (Gentner) made the sound of flying bees' wings; Marcus told us that he knew where the comma was on a certain page; Johnny said, "I heard a rhyme!"; and Tonya noticed that the last name of the author of the poem "Cats" was *Katz*, which was pronounced the same.

I was intrigued by the wide variety of student input. They were all free to contribute at their own literacy level and interest because they knew that I was not looking for a specific answer. The students were validated and encouraged to continue to notice language and illustrations in every text they encountered. I was also able to learn more about individual children based on what they shared. An informal yet useful assessment tool could emerge from jotting down each "I notice" and noting how each individual's input changes and progresses over the year. I also realized that through the children's contributions we covered many of our school and state grade re-quirements for communication skills.

Mystery Letter

I decided to create a pen pal for my students as a way to address letter format and other literacy skills and strategies. One day during shared reading I brought in a letter on chart paper written by my puppet, "Miss Compassion." (I got the idea for Miss Compassion from my mother, who has a puppet named Ms. Kindness.) She introduced herself and indicated that she wanted to correspond with the group. The students initially wanted to know who *really* wrote the letter, but they were soon able to suspend their disbelief and have fun with it.

Some of Miss Compassion's letters included an envelope with a question in it. The questions were either explicit, such as "How many words are there in my note?" or "List some of the synonyms for my name," or they asked the students to share, such as "Tell the person next to you something you are good at doing."

The students were engaged, and we were able to generate a lot of discussion around the Miss Compassion letters. I treated the questions from Miss Compassion as language games, not tests, and observed how the students reacted and participated. When the group was not interested in the question, I put the letter away and moved on to a book, song, or poem. I did not want to turn the Mystery Letter into a drill.

Nonfiction Texts

We explore nonfiction books in a different way. Before reading, I flip the pages of the book and ask students to keep in mind what they notice as the pages go by. The variety of responses amazes me. In order to illustrate that we do not have to read a nonfiction book from cover to cover, we select from the table of contents a section that looks interesting, find the page it is on, and read just that section.

I use nonfiction big books to address some of the subject matter in my curriculum, and to address study skills, such as reading table of contents, indexes, graphs, charts, and labels. The students are learning these things in the context of reading for meaning. For example, we began reading *Warming Up! Cooling Off!* (Cutting) by skimming the pages first, to get a feel for the contents. Then I showed them the table of contents and had one student choose an area he wanted to read more about. I pointed to the particular section and followed my hand across to the page number. We located the page in the book and read. As we read, I commented on the labels that point to pictures. The class together read the graphs to learn more information. After a few days with the same book, we turned to the index to find material that we wanted to review.

The students use the information books in their follow-up time to find more information for animal comparisons or projects or to create their own information book. They learn to read the tables of contents and the indexes in order to find what they need in a book. We routinely refer to those areas of nonfiction books so that it becomes natural and necessary for students to know how to use them.

There are many opportunities for math concepts to be incorporated into shared reading, with or without a specific "math" text. When we worked with a nonfiction text that contained a table of contents and an index, we explored chapters and topics in a different order than the text was written. This allowed me to include a mini-lesson without disrupting the overall meaning. With the text *Warming Up! Cooling Off!* (Cutting) I asked, "Is page 3 going to be near the beginning or end of the book?" "How can we get to page 25 without going page by page from the beginning?" "Using the index, how can we tell what topic is going to be covered before 'Babies'?" or "Looking at the table of contents, how do we know how many pages the chapter on 'Exploring and Hiding' is going to be?"

End Song
The students choose our ending song from among our collection of familiar charts and books. We often find time for a song or two. This singing is joyful, relaxed, and simply a fun time to enjoy a text together. Popular follow-up activities for songs include using charts and pointers to read, copying and illustrating songs from our class songbook, listening to the songbook tapes, and singing from the big books.

Read Aloud
I often read aloud from a trade book to end many sessions. We have sung and enthusiastically worked for a good part of the morning, so

I feel this is a perfect time to relax in a bedtime story manner. Not all students are read to at home, and stories are a soothing way to end our session quietly while continuing to engage in important literacy. I select books that are great stories, that have particular relevance to a content area we are covering, or that are suggested to me by the students.

I usually highlight the author and illustrator, especially if it is a favorite of mine. The students enjoy seeing books autographed by the author or illustrator, so I try to get books signed at conferences. The day I ended with *The Island of the Skog* (Kellogg), several students searched the library for other books by Kellogg. A few children found books that he had illustrated but had not written. They were able to recognize and identify his style of drawing.

Shared Reading and Testing

I started teaching at a time when standards and testing were becoming an integral part of the curriculum, and I can't ignore the reality that they play in my life as a teacher. I have found, however, that through shared reading I can teach many of the skills that my students meet on the tests and at the same time maintain an atmosphere where children learn to read and love to read.

Part of successful test taking is being familiar with the test format, so I designed paper and pencil "tests" on the areas that my curriculum requires. These "test ready" sheets are in test format, and I use the same wording and design as the students will see during testing week. Not only does this expose them to the test format but it shows me whom I need to check with about certain concepts. For example, "Do they understand how to use the table of contents but not how to answer paper-and-pencil questions about it? Do we need to discuss the settings of our texts in greater detail?" The "test ready" sheets show the students what their real life experiences look like when stripped down to contextless test items.

To begin, I listed the skills and concepts that comprise my state standards, and divided the list into sections: oral communication, reading strategies, and literature. I divided these sections further into each specific standard that I must teach. I write the date and any notes next to the particular standard on my lists, and periodically review my lists to ensure that I am covering all of the standards. While I do choose the texts for the meaning and content, I am also aware of which skills and concepts I can best teach using particular texts. In other words, I find a text I want to use and determine which standards to focus on. Since we reread our big books and charts, there are many opportunities to address different standards with one text as well as review them regularly.

I continually discuss words that the students will later use to talk about their own writing, as well as those that I know the students will need to know for testing. By using the vocabulary in context, the students become comfortable and familiar with such phrases and concepts as "setting," "takes place," "good title," "problem," "solution," "solved," "happens next," "characters," and "passage."

Shared reading invites us to learn about language by using language in the context of stories and meaningful texts. My goal is to keep our discussions and learning purposeful and relevant so my students will learn to love reading as they learn to read.

Appendixes

Reproducible Forms

Name_____Date_____

STORYBOOK PLAN

TITLE _____

CHARACTERS _____

PLACE _____

TIME _____

MOOD _____

Figure A–1   Storybook Plan

Figure A-2 Masks

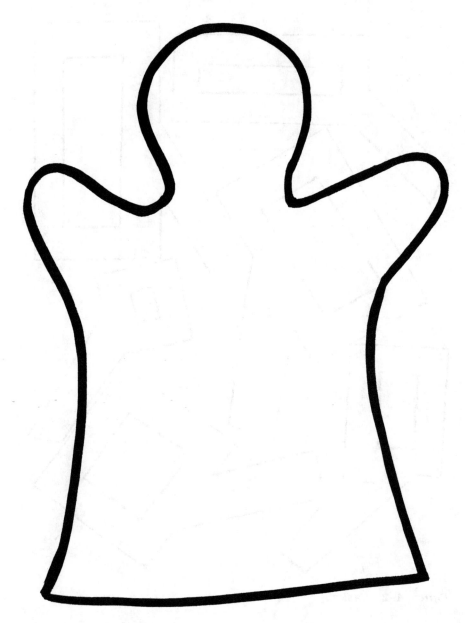

Figure A-3 Puppet

	Monday	Tuesday	Wednesday	Thursday	Friday
Warm Ups: <u>song poem chart</u>					
<u>New</u> Type:					
Other/old					
Focus + skills					
Notes					
Read Aloud					

Figure A-4 Planning Form

Children's Books
Mentioned in the Text

Aylesworth, Jim. 1992. *Old Black Fly*. New York: Henry Holt.

Arnold, Tedd. 1987. *No More Jumping on the Bed*. New York: Dial.

Belanger, Claude. 1988. *The Circus Is in Town*. Crystal Lake, IL: Rigby.

Blanchard, Pat, and Joanne Suhr. 1997. *Itch! Itch!* Greenvale, NY: Mondo.

Brown, Ruth. 1947. *Goodnight Moon*. New York: Harper Row.

Cowley, Joy. 1998. *The Scrubbing Machine*. Bothell, WA: The Wright Group.

———. 1980. *Hairy Bear*. Bothell, WA: The Wright Group.

Cowley, Joy, and June Melser. 1980. *In a Dark, Dark Wood*. Bothell, WA: The Wright Group.

Cutting, Brian, and Jilian Cutting. 1993. *Warming Up! Cooling Off!* Bothell, WA: The Wright Group.

Daniel, Alan, and Lea Daniel, illus. 1990. *Down by the Bay*. Bothell, WA: The Wright Group.

———. 1990. *Old MacDonald Had a Farm*. Bothell, WA: The Wright Group.

Drew, David. 1987. *Tadpole Diary*. Crystal Lake, IL: Rigby.

Eastman, P. D. 1960. *Are You My Mother?* New York: Random House.

Gentner, Norma. 1995. *Busy Bees*. Bothell, WA: The Wright Group.

———. 1995. *Frog on a Log*. Bothell, WA: The Wright Group.

———. 1995. *The Predator*. Bothell, WA: The Wright Group.

———. 1993. *Bear Facts*. Bothell, WA: The Wright Group.

———. 1993. *Munch, Munch, Munch*. Bothell, WA: The Wright Group.

Harwayne, Shelley. 1995. *Jewels*. Greenvale, NY: Mondo.

Hayes, Sarah. 1995. *This Is the Bear*. Big Book Edition. Cambridge, MA: Candlewick Press.

Johnson, JoAnne. 1998. *Picture Perfect Word Book*. Carmel, CA: Hampton-Brown.

Kaufman, William. 1991. *Catch Me the Moon Daddy*. Crystal Lake, IL: Rigby.

Kellogg, Steven. 1973. *The Island of the Skog*. New York: Dial Press.

Munsch, Robert. 1983. *Mortimer*. Toronto: Annick Press.

Parkes, Brenda. 1998. *Crunchy Munchy*. Crystal Lake, IL: Rigby.

———. 1989. *Goodnight, Goodnight*. Crystal Lake, IL: Rigby.

————. 1985. *The Three Little Pigs*. Crystal Lake, IL: Rigby.

Parkes, Brenda, and Judith Smith. 1984. *The Gingerbread Man*. Crystal Lake, IL: Rigby.

Phinney, Margaret Y. 1994. *Exploring Land Habitats*. Greenvale, NY: Mondo.

Plater, Inge. 1997. *Jolly Olly*. Crystal Lake, IL: Rigby.

Robinson, Vicki. 1993. *Our Eyes*. Bothell, WA: The Wright Group.

Rohman, Cricket. 1996. *The Queen Made a Quilt*. Thousand Oaks, CA: Outside the Box, Inc.

Sendak, Maurice. 1963. *Where the Wild Things Are*. New York: Harper.

Snowball, Diane. 1995. *Chickens*. Greenvale, NY: Mondo.

Taberski, Sharon. 1996. *Morning, Noon, and Night: Poems to Fill Your Day*. Greenvale, NY: Mondo.

Traynor, Pamela. 1997. *Hiking in the* U.S.A. Crystal Lake, IL: Rigby.

Wilde, Buck. 1997. *Journey to the Sea: The Snake River*. Crystal Lake, IL: Rigby.

References

Cambourne, Brian. 1988. *The Whole Story*. New York: Scholastic.

Clay, Marie. 1993. *An Observational Survey of Early Literacy Achievement*. Portsmouth, NH: Heinemann.

Fisher, Bobbi. 1998. *Joyful Learning in Kindergarten, Revised Edition*. Portsmouth, NH: Heinemann.

———. 1996. *Inside the Classroom: Teaching Kindergarten and First Grade*. Portsmouth, NH: Heinemann.

———. 1995. *Thinking and Learning Together: Curriculum and Community in a Primary Classroom*. Portsmouth, NH: Heinemann.

———. 1994. *Classroom Close-up: Bobbi Fisher: Organization and Management*. Bothell, WA: The Wright Group. Videotape.

Holdaway, Don. 1979. *Foundations of Literacy*. Portsmouth, NH: Heinemann.

Moustafa, Margaret. 1997. *Beyond Traditional Phonics*. Portsmouth, NH: Heinemann.